I DECLARE I WILL
not let anyone steal
my crown. I am a

radiant

child of God and I know
I can do and achieve many things

I DECLARE

that I am

blessed

in so many different
areas of my life

Even when I do not see it
or feel it, I will still state it and

believe it

THIS JOURNAL BELONGS TO

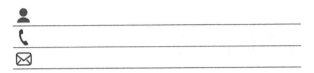

Words and illustration
by Antoinette Fatih

Dear Beautiful You

This little notebook is here to encourage and empower you every single day!

We know that some days might be a challenge - people might try to steal your glory or your joy. But this gives you a daily reminder that you were made to sparkle! So don't let anybody steal your crown - that is, your authority, your happiness or good favour.

I hope you love your new notebook. It's a place for you to write down those dreams you treasure in your heart.

The thoughts we have are powerful - without realising it, they become imprinted in our minds. So on each page I have created a powerful affirmation to motivate, uplift and inspire you!

Enjoy using your journal, my lovely - and have fun...

Antoinette xxx

PS. Visit us at antoinettefaith.com/freebie and **you can get a free and helpful gift as a thank you...**

www.AntoinetteFaith.com

I won't let anybody steal my crown...

....
....
....
....
....
....
....
....
....
....
....
....
....
....
....
....
....
....

Did you keep hold of your crown today?

Yes! Sort of...! Um..no...

I declare that I
have a joyful heart,
my mind is strong.
I see new mercies
daily and my days
are filled with
wonderful
possibilities

I won't let anybody steal my crown...

....

....

....

....

....

....

....

....

....

....

....

....

....

....

....

....

....

....

Did you keep hold of your crown today?

Yes!   Sort of...!   Um..no...

I DECLARE THAT I SPEAK

healing & good health

to my entire body

I REALISE MY BODY IS

precious

and I treat it with kindness,
respect and love

I won't let anybody steal my crown...

....
....
....
....
....
....
....
....
....
....
....
....
....
....
....
....
....
....
....
....

Did you keep hold of your crown today?

Yes!

Sort of...!

Um..no...

I DECLARE THAT EVEN

when things don't go exactly as I planned

I remain blessed

because God holds me in his hands

I won't let anybody steal my crown...

....

....

....

....

....

....

....

....

....

....

....

....

....

....

....

....

....

....

....

....

Did you keep hold of your crown today?

Yes!   Sort of...!   Um..no...

I DECLARE THAT I AM
INTELLIGENT
resourceful and

creative

I am self-disciplined

I KNOW THAT EVERY
SUCCESSFUL PERSON

practises self-discipline and

I will do the same

I won't let anybody steal my crown...

....

....

....

....

....

....

....

....

....

....

....

....

....

....

....

....

....

....

Did you keep hold of your crown today?

Yes!   Sort of...!   Um..no...

I DECLARE THAT I WILL FACE EACH DAY WITH

positive expectations

*Even when challenges come my way,
I know that God is there to comfort
me in times of need*

I won't let anybody steal my crown...

....

....

....

....

....

....

....

....

....

....

....

....

....

....

....

....

....

....

....

....

Did you keep hold of your crown today?

Yes!

Sort of...!

Um..no...

I declare that God has placed many dreams and plans in my heart.

They are there for a reason

I know if I take the right action now then in the right season they will become a reality

I won't let anybody steal my crown...

....
....
....
....
....
....
....
....
....
....
....
....
....
....
....
....
....
....
....

Did you keep hold of your crown today?

Yes!

Sort of...!

Um..no...

I DECLARE THAT

all things work to the good

I know that with God

ALL THINGS ARE POSSIBLE

so I move forward with confidence

in the direction of my dreams

I won't let anybody steal my crown...

....

....

....

....

....

....

....

....

....

....

....

....

....

....

....

....

....

....

....

Did you keep hold of your crown today?

Yes!   Sort of...!   Um..no...

I DECLARE THAT ALONGSIDE

my prayers

I also take action

I KNOW THAT

positive action

is necessary for any

DREAMS OR PLANS TO COME

true

I won't let anybody steal my crown...

....
....
....
....
....
....
....
....
....
....
....
....
....
....
....
....
....
....
....
....

Did you keep hold of your crown today?

Yes!   Sort of...!   Um..no...

I DECLARE THAT EVEN WHEN
OTHERS DON'T BELIEVE IN ME,
I STILL BELIEVE IN MYSELF -
AND THAT MAKES ME A

champion

I won't let anybody steal my crown...

....

....

....

....

....

....

....

....

....

....

....

....

....

....

....

....

....

....

....

....

Did you keep hold of your crown today?

Yes!   Sort of...!   Um..no...

I DECLARE

that I am a

WOMAN OF COURAGE

A WOMAN OF DISCIPLINE

and a

WOMAN OF HOPE

I won't let anybody steal my crown...

....
....
....
....
....
....
....
....
....
....
....
....
....
....
....
....
....
....

Did you keep hold of your crown today?

Yes!   Sort of...!   Um..no...

I DECLARE THAT I CHOOSE
to be happy and joyful

- whatever I do
I do with confidence
and expectation that
good results will follow

I won't let anybody steal my crown...

....
....
....
....
....
....
....
....
....
....
....
....
....
....
....
....
....
....
....
....

Did you keep hold of your crown today?

Yes!

Sort of...!

Um..no...

I DECLARE THAT

I make the best

*of the positive opportunities that
are presented to me*

I won't let anybody steal my crown...

....
....
....
....
....
....
....
....
....
....
....
....
....
....
....
....
....
....

Did you keep hold of your crown today?

Yes!　　　　Sort of...!　　　Um..no...

I declare that I will look
for the good in other
people
- and know when to give
them the benefit of the
doubt
- expecting them to
extend the same
courtesy to me

I won't let anybody steal my crown...

....
....
....
....
....
....
....
....
....
....
....
....
....
....
....
....
....
....
....

Did you keep hold of your crown today?

Yes!   Sort of...!   Um..no...

I DECLARE THAT I AM A SUCCESS

GOD HAS BLESSED ME

WITH THE ABILITY TO

TRIUMPH

OVER ANY DIFFICULTIES

I won't let anybody steal my crown...

....

....

....

....

....

....

....

....

....

....

....

....

....

....

....

....

....

....

....

Did you keep hold of your crown today?

Yes!   Sort of...!   Um..no...

I DECLARE

that when anyone compliments me
I am able to say

THANK YOU

and accept it graciously

I won't let anybody steal my crown...

....
....
....
....
....
....
....
....
....
....
....
....
....
....
....
....
....
....
....

Did you keep hold of your crown today?

Yes!   Sort of...!   Um..no...

I declare that even when I
experience setbacks they
are just temporary

I know a test comes
before a testimony. I will
keep on moving and
comeback

I won't let anybody steal my crown...

....

....

....

....

....

....

....

....

....

....

....

....

....

....

....

....

....

....

Did you keep hold of your crown today?

Yes!

Sort of...!

Um..no...

I DECLARE THAT THE

great dreams

that have been placed in my
heart are there for a good reason

AND BECAUSE OF THAT THEY ARE

destined

to become a reality

I won't let anybody steal my crown...

....
....
....
....
....
....
....
....
....
....
....
....
....
....
....
....
....
....
....
....
....
....

Did you keep hold of your crown today?

Yes!   Sort of...!   Um..no...

I DECLARE THAT GOD IS WITH ME

I will not fail

I won't let anybody steal my crown...

....

....

....

....

....

....

....

....

....

....

....

....

....

....

....

....

....

....

Did you keep hold of your crown today?

Yes!   Sort of...!   Um..no...

I DECLARE

I have a

positive mind

as I need a positive mind to
lead a positive life

I won't let anybody steal my crown...

....

....

....

....

....

....

....

....

....

....

....

....

....

....

....

....

....

....

....

Did you keep hold of your crown today?

Yes!   Sort of...!   Um..no...

I DECLARE
THAT I AM
CALM, PATIENT
AND RESILIENT
- EVEN IN
TIMES OF
STRESS

I won't let anybody steal my crown...

....
....
....
....
....
....
....
....
....
....
....
....
....
....
....
....
....
....
....
....

Did you keep hold of your crown today?

Yes!

Sort of...!

Um..no...

I DECLARE THAT

God loves me

just the way I am

I AM A

beautiful creation

from the crown of my head
to the soles of my feet

I won't let anybody steal my crown...

....

....

....

....

....

....

....

....

....

....

....

....

....

....

....

....

....

....

....

Did you keep hold of your crown today?

Yes!

Sort of...!

Um..no...

I DECLARE THERE IS
A PURPOSE TO MY LIFE

I am focused and
whatever I put my
mind to

I ACCOMPLISH

I won't let anybody steal my crown...

....
....
....
....
....
....
....
....
....
....
....
....
....
....
....
....
....
....
....
....
....

Did you keep hold of your crown today?

Yes!   Sort of...!   Um..no...

I declare that
there are many
kindhearted people
I meet in my life's
journey - I am
grateful to all
those who have
helped me along
the way

I won't let anybody steal my crown...

....
....
....
....
....
....
....
....
....
....
....
....
....
....
....
....
....
....
....

Did you keep hold of your crown today?

Yes!

Sort of...!

Um..no...

I DECLARE

that I use

positive words to myself

I will speak words of compassion, that
uplift and empower me - speaking with
confidence into my situation

I won't let anybody steal my crown...

....

....

....

....

....

....

....

....

....

....

....

....

....

....

....

....

....

....

....

Did you keep hold of your crown today?

Yes!   Sort of...!   Um..no...

I DECLARE
I won't dwell on the stress!
I will focus on higher things
and say

I am blessed

I won't let anybody steal my crown...

....

....

....

....

....

....

....

....

....

....

....

....

....

....

....

....

....

....

....

Did you keep hold of your crown today?

Yes!　　　　Sort of...!　　　Um..no...

I declare
that with God's help
I am strong enough to
overcome
any obstacles

I won't let anybody steal my crown...

....

....

....

....

....

....

....

....

....

....

....

....

....

....

....

....

....

....

....

....

Did you keep hold of your crown today?

Yes!

Sort of...!

Um..no...

I declare that I am blessed
WITH A SOUND MIND

AND I NOURISH MY MIND
BY READING BOOKS THAT

uplift, motivate
and inspire

I won't let anybody steal my crown...

....
....
....
....
....
....
....
....
....
....
....
....
....
....
....
....
....
....
....

Did you keep hold of your crown today?

Yes!

Sort of...!

Um..no...

I DECLARE THAT

love is powerful

kindness prevails

AND IT IS A POWERFUL ACT TO BOTH

forgive

and receive forgivness

I won't let anybody steal my crown...

....
....
....
....
....
....
....
....
....
....
....
....
....
....
....
....
....
....

Did you keep hold of your crown today?

Yes! Sort of...! Um..no...

I DECLARE THAT I USE THE

KNOWLEDGE

THAT I'VE ACQUIRED

I AM LIKE A RIVER THAT KEEPS

FLOWING

AND NOT A POND THAT STAGNATES.

WHAT I LEARN,

I SHARE

WITH OTHERS

I won't let anybody steal my crown...

....

....

....

....

....

....

....

....

....

....

....

....

....

....

....

....

....

....

....

....

Did you keep hold of your crown today?

Yes!   Sort of...!   Um..no...

I DECLARE THAT I MAKE
TIME FOR

REST & RENEWAL

I KNOW THOSE TIMES ARE
VITAL FOR

MY MIND, MY BODY
& MY SPIRIT

I won't let anybody steal my crown...

....

....

....

....

....

....

....

....

....

....

....

....

....

....

....

....

....

....

Did you keep hold of your crown today?

Yes!   Sort of...!   Um..no...

I DECLARE THAT

I am

victorious

I grow more confident and
stronger every day

I won't let anybody steal my crown...

....
....
....
....
....
....
....
....
....
....
....
....
....
....
....
....
....
....
....
....

Did you keep hold of your crown today?

Yes!   Sort of...!   Um..no...

I DECLARE THAT GOD
HAS GIVEN ME

MANY SKILLS
AND TALENTS

I WILL FIND THE PLACE

FOR ME TO SHINE

AND USE

MY TALENTS THERE

I won't let anybody steal my crown...

....
....
....
....
....
....
....
....
....
....
....
....
....
....
....
....
....
....

Did you keep hold of your crown today?

Yes!   Sort of...!   Um..no...

I DECLARE

I am blessed financially
I am blessed

abundantly

and I use my blessings to help others

I won't let anybody steal my crown...

....

....

....

....

....

....

....

....

....

....

....

....

....

....

....

....

....

....

Did you keep hold of your crown today?

Yes!

Sort of...!

Um..no...

I declare that even if I don't feel it

I AM STRONG

I won't let anybody steal my crown...

....
....
....
....
....
....
....
....
....
....
....
....
....
....
....
....
....
....
....
....

Did you keep hold of your crown today?

Yes!

Sort of...!

Um..no...

I DECLARE THAT

I am kind to other people
I declare

love, blessings
& harmony

on my friends,
family and neighbourhood

I won't let anybody steal my crown...

....
....
....
....
....
....
....
....
....
....
....
....
....
....
....
....
....
....
....
....

Did you keep hold of your crown today?

Yes!   Sort of...!   Um..no...

I DECLARE THAT

my home is a blessing

a haven of comfort, peace and calm

I won't let anybody steal my crown...

....
....
....
....
....
....
....
....
....
....
....
....
....
....
....
....
....
....

Did you keep hold of your crown today?

Yes!

Sort of...!

Um..no...

I DECLARE THAT I AM NOT LIMITED BY
THE LIMITATIONS OTHERS PLACE ON ME

I know
my value & my worth

I know that I am able to
do many things

I won't let anybody steal my crown...

....
....
....
....
....
....
....
....
....
....
....
....
....
....
....
....
....
....
....
....

Did you keep hold of your crown today?

Yes!

Sort of...!

Um..no...

I DECLARE THAT I
do not need to seek the praise
of other people.

I let my effort

speak for itself

I won't let anybody steal my crown...

....
....
....
....
....
....
....
....
....
....
....
....
....
....
....
....
....
....
....
....

Did you keep hold of your crown today?

Yes!

Sort of...!

Um..no...

I declare that I am a woman
with
love in her heart
determination in her mind
and courage in her soul

I am a woman who encourages
others

-AND HERSELF

I won't let anybody steal my crown...

....

....

....

....

....

....

....

....

....

....

....

....

....

....

....

....

....

....

Did you keep hold of your crown today?

Yes!   Sort of...!   Um..no...

I DECLARE THAT I AM

patient

I am disciplined and strong
I DO NOT GIVE UP AT THE FIRST SIGN
OF DIFFICULTY. I KNOW OUT OF THE
MISTAKES OF LIFE THERE IS OFTEN
A MESSAGE

I persevere

and reach my goals

I won't let anybody steal my crown...

....

....

....

....

....

....

....

....

....

....

....

....

....

....

....

....

....

....

....

Did you keep hold of your crown today?

Yes!   Sort of...!   Um..no...

I declare that I realise time is precious

- and my days are a gift to be treasured and valued

I won't let anybody steal my crown...

....
....
....
....
....
....
....
....
....
....
....
....
....
....
....
....
....
....
....

Did you keep hold of your crown today?

Yes!   Sort of...!   Um..no...

I declare that I am

CAPABLE

of learning from my experiences. I declare that I am blessed with the

WISDOM

not to make the same mistakes again and again and again

I won't let anybody steal my crown...

....
....
....
....
....
....
....
....
....
....
....
....
....
....
....
....
....
....
....

Did you keep hold of your crown today?

Yes!

Sort of...!

Um..no...

I DECLARE

I am strong and courageous

God is with me

wherever I go

I won't let anybody steal my crown...

....

....

....

....

....

....

....

....

....

....

....

....

....

....

....

....

....

....

....

Did you keep hold of your crown today?

Yes!   Sort of...!   Um..no...

I DECLARE I USE SOME OF MY
TIME AND RESOURCES TO

BE A HELP

TO OTHERS

I won't let anybody steal my crown...

....

....

....

....

....

....

....

....

....

....

....

....

....

....

....

....

....

....

....

....

Did you keep hold of your crown today?

Yes!   Sort of...!   Um..no...

I DECLARE I CAN DO ALL
THINGS THROUGH
CHRIST WHO
GIVES ME STRENGTH

I won't let anybody steal my crown...

....
....
....
....
....
....
....
....
....
....
....
....
....
....
....
....
....
....
....

Did you keep hold of your crown today?

Yes!   Sort of...!   Um..no...

I DECLARE I WILL NOT STAGNATE

I WILL KEEP

moving forward

- GRATEFUL FOR THE LESSONS

I LEARN ALONG THE WAY

I won't let anybody steal my crown...

....
....
....
....
....
....
....
....
....
....
....
....
....
....
....
....
....
....
....

Did you keep hold of your crown today?

Yes!   Sort of...!   Um..no...

I DECLARE ANY CHALLENGES
I FACE ARE REALLY

OPPORTUNITIES TO LEARN & GROW

They enable me to discover and use
skills that I didn't realise I had

I won't let anybody steal my crown...

....
....
....
....
....
....
....
....
....
....
....
....
....
....
....
....
....
....

Did you keep hold of your crown today?

Yes!   Sort of...!   Um..no...

I DECLARE MY LIFE IS OPEN
TO MEETING OTHERS
WITH KNOWLEDGE AND EXPERIENCE

I am able to learn from them

They have a positive impact on my life and I have a positive impact on them

I won't let anybody steal my crown...

....
....
....
....
....
....
....
....
....
....
....
....
....
....
....
....
....
....
....

Did you keep hold of your crown today?

Yes...   Sort of...   Um... no

I DECLARE THAT

I am able to use my experiences to

help other people

I use my words to lift others up
and not to bring them down

I won't let anybody steal my crown...

....
....
....
....
....
....
....
....
....
....
....
....
....
....
....
....
....
....
....

Did you keep hold of your crown today?

Yes...

Sort of...

Um... no

I DECLARE

I know and am fulfilling

my life's purpose

I am moving in the right direction
- with a life that is full of value and meaning

I won't let anybody steal my crown...

....
....
....
....
....
....
....
....
....
....
....
....
....
....
....
....
....
....
....
....

Did you keep hold of your crown today?

Yes...

Sort of...

Um... no

I DECLARE THAT I AM

creative

able to think of new and
flexible solutions to those
challenges I might face

I won't let anybody steal my crown...

....

....

....

....

....

....

....

....

....

....

....

....

....

....

....

....

....

....

....

Did you keep hold of your crown today?

Yes...   Sort of...   Um... no

I declare that I am organised.
I tackle projects in a timely manner and

get things done
when they need to be done

I do my best to maintain a positive
and cheerful attitude

I won't let anybody steal my crown...

....
....
....
....
....
....
....
....
....
....
....
....
....
....
....
....
....
....
....

Did you keep hold of your crown today?

Yes...   Sort of...   Um... no

I DECLARE MY HEART IS

open and excited

about the different possibilities that come my way

I won't let anybody steal my crown...

....

....

....

....

....

....

....

....

....

....

....

....

....

....

....

....

....

....

....

Did you keep hold of your crown today?

Yes...

Sort of...

Um... no

I DECLARE THAT I AM

resilient

- physically and emotionally strong
and able to bounce
back from challenges

I won't let anybody steal my crown...

....

....

....

....

....

....

....

....

....

....

....

....

....

....

....

....

....

....

Did you keep hold of your crown today?

Yes!   Sort of...   Um... no

I DECLARE THAT I PRACTICE

COMPASSION & KINDNESS

JUST AS I EXPECT OTHERS TO PRACTICE
KINDNESS & COMPASSION WITH ME

I won't let anybody steal my crown...

....
....
....
....
....
....
....
....
....
....
....
....
....
....
....
....
....
....
....

Did you keep hold of your crown today?

Yes... Sort of... Um... no

I DECLARE THAT I RECOGNISE THAT OUR
ENVIRONMENT IS

SPECIAL

*I am careful of the resources that I use
and I take time to appreciate the beauty of nature*

I won't let anybody steal my crown...

....
....
....
....
....
....
....
....
....
....
....
....
....
....
....
....
....
....
....
....

Did you keep hold of your crown today?

Yes!   Sort of...   Um... no

I DECLARE

that I have a

loving heart

I am surrounded by love and able to express
gratitude and appreciation

I AM ABLE
to compliment those around me

My soul is full of

love & peace

I won't let anybody steal my crown...

....

....

....

....

....

....

....

....

....

....

....

....

....

....

....

....

....

....

....

Did you keep hold of your crown today?

Yes!   Sort of...   Um... no

I DECLARE
my days will be full with

praise

and thanksgiving.
I will remember to express gratitude
for even the smallest of
things - as these often turn out
to be the most important things of all